P9-DMZ-558

HAWKEYE COLLINS & AMY ADAMS in

THE CASE OF THE
CHOCOLATE
SNATCHER
& OTHER MYSTERIES

by M. MASTERS

Meadowbrook Press
18318 Minnetonka Blvd.
Deephaven, MN 55391

This book is dedicated to all the children across the country who helped us develop the *Can You Solve the Mystery?*™ series.

Second Printing July 1983

Library of Congress Cataloging in Publication Data

Masters, M.
Hawkeye Collins and Amy Adams in the case of the chocolate snatcher and other mysteries.

At head of title: Can you solve the mystery?
Summary: Nine short mysteries starring Hawkeye Collins and Amy Adams, two twelve-year-old sleuths who solve mysteries using Hawkeye's sketches of important clues. The reader is invited to solve the mystery before the solution is presented.
[1. Mystery and detective stories. 2. Literary recreations.] I. Title.
II. Title: Case of the chocolate snatcher and other mysteries.
PZ7.M42392Haw   1983   [Fic]   83-848

ISBN 0-915658-85-2

Printed in the United States of America

ISBN (Paperback) 0-915658-85-2

Copyright © 1983 by Lansky & Associates.

All stories written by Alexander von Wacker.
Illustrations by Stephen Cardot.

Editor: Kathe Grooms
Assistant Editor: Louise Delagran
Design: Stephen Cardot, Terry Dugan
Production: John Ware, Donna Ahrens, Pamela Barnard
Cover Art: Tom Foty

CONTENTS

Amy Adams   Hawkeye Collins

Young Sleuths Detect Fun in Mysteries

By Alice Cory
Staff Writer

Lakewood Hills has two new super sleuths watching over its citizens. They are Christoper "Hawkeye" Collins and Amy Amanda Adams, both 12 years old and sixth-grade students at Lakewood Hills Elementary.

Christopher Collins, the popular, blond, blue-eyed sleuth of 128 Crestview Drive, is better known by his nickname, "Hawkeye." His father, Peter Collins, who is an attorney downtown, explains, "We started calling him Hawkeye many years ago because he notices everything, even tiny details. That's what makes him so good at solving mysteries." His mother, Linda Collins, a real estate agent, agrees: "Yes, but he

Sleuths continued on page 4A

Sleuths continued from page 2A

also started to draw at a very early age. His sketches capture everything he sees. He draws clues or the scene of the crime — or anything else that will help solve a mystery."

Amy Adams, a spitfire with red hair and sparkling green eyes, lives right across the street, at 131 Crestview Drive. Known to many as the star of the track team, she is also a star math student. "She's quick of mind, quick of foot and quick of temper," says her teacher, Ted Bronson, chuckling. "And she's never intimidated." Not only do she and Hawkeye share the same birthday, but also the same love of mysteries.

"If something's wrong," says Amy, leaning on her ten-speed, "you just can't look the other way."

"Right," says Hawkeye, pulling his ever-present sketch pad and pencil from his back pocket. "And if we can't solve a case right away, I'll do a drawing of the scene of the crime. When we study my sketch, we can usually figure out what happened."

When the two detectives are not playing video games or soccer (Hawkeye is the captain of the sixth-grade team), they can often be seen biking around town, making sure justice is done. Occa-

sionally aided by Hawkeye's frisky golden retriever, Nosey, and Amy's six-year-old sister, Lucy, they've solved every case they've handled to date.

How did the two get started in the detective business?

It all started last year at Lakewood Hills Elementary's Career Days. There the two met Sergeant Treadwell, one of Lakewood Hills' best-known policemen. Of Hawkeye and Amy, Sergeant Treadwell proudly brags, "They're terrific. Right after we met, one of the teachers had a whole pile of tests stolen. I sure couldn't figure out who had done it, but Hawkeye did one of his sketches and he and Amy had the case solved in five minutes! You can't fool those two."

Sergeant Treadwell adds: "I don't know what Lakewood Hills ever did without Hawkeye and Amy. They've found a dognapped dog, located stolen video games, and cracked many other tough cases. Why, whenever I have a problem I can't solve, I know just where to go — straight to those two super sleuths!"

> **" They've found a dognapped dog, located stolen video games, and cracked many other tough cases. "**

Ends Today!
SAL

Dear Readers,

You can solve these mysteries along with us! Start by reading very carefully -- Watch out for things like what people say happened, the ways they behave, and details like the time and the weather.

Then look closely at the sketch or other picture clue with the story. If you remember the facts, the picture clue should help you break the case.

If you want to check your answer -- or if a hard case stumps you -- turn to the solutions at the back of the book. They're written in mirror type. Hold them up to a mirror and they'll look right. If you don't have a mirror, turn the page and hold it up to the light. (You can teach yourself to read backwards, too. We can do it pretty well now and it comes in handy some- times in our cases.)

Have fun -- we sure did!

Amy

Hawkeye

The Case of the Crashing Candelabrum

The telephone wasn't even halfway through the first ring when Nosey started barking and prancing.

"I got it!" called Hawkeye to his mother, a real estate agent, who was meeting with a client in the living room.

Nosey, wriggling all over, stepped cautiously up to the ringing phone.

"Okay, Nosey," said Hawkeye. "Answer the phone. Go on, get it. Answer the phone."

With big, brown eyes, Nosey glanced up at Hawkeye, then at the phone. She stuck her nose out, sniffed, and, finally, she very gently picked up the receiver in her mouth.

1

"Good girl, Nosey! That's great. Now give it to me. Give . . ."

Before Hawkeye could grab it, the dog dropped the receiver on the floor, where it landed with a crash. Hawkeye slapped his forehead and scooped up the phone at once.

"Hello? Hello?" said Hawkeye loudly. "Is anyone there?"

It was several seconds before his father's voice came over the line.

"Ow, my ear. That hurt. Hawkeye, what in the heck did you do? Throw the phone out the window?"

"Dad. Oh, hi." Hawkeye hoped he wouldn't get in trouble. "Sorry. I've been teaching Nosey a neat trick this afternoon. When the phone rings, she runs over and answers it. That's so that if a burglar or robber calls when we're not home—you know, to case our house— it'll seem like someone's here."

"Well, let me know when you get Nosey to talk, okay? That's going to be the hard part." Mr. Collins, swiveling in his big chair in his law office downtown, chortled at his own joke.

"Anyway, enough with the detective stuff. Is your mother there? I just wanted to tell her I'll be a little late tonight."

"She's in the living room with Mrs. Fields. They're looking for a house for some

2

friends of Mrs. Fields who are moving into town."

"Well, don't interrupt them. Would you give her the message?"

"Sure, Dad."

"And, Hawkeye, shouldn't you be doing your math?"

"Aw, Dad, I'm doing fine in math. I just don't like to study it."

"Well," said Mr. Collins firmly, "if you only put a little time into it, you'd do just as well at math as you do in computer programming. Not to mention video games and soccer."

Hawkeye scratched his blonde hair in discomfort. "Oh, all right."

"After dinner, let's put in some time debugging your spaghetti and meatballs video game, okay? I think you've just about got it."

Hawkeye brightened. "Me, too. It's going to be a terrific game once I get the meatballs to roll all over the screen. Let's start right after supper."

"Okay, see you later. Bye."

When Hawkeye relayed the message later, his mother asked him to help Mrs. Fields carry some real estate books to her house.

"Mrs. Fields is going to borrow them overnight to look over the pictures of houses," said Mrs. Collins. "Would you help her carry them out, dear? Otherwise, she'll have to make a couple of trips."

"Will do, Mom," said Hawkeye. "I'll take Nosey with me."

Hawkeye sat on the floor in the hallway and put on his running shoes.

"Here," said Mrs. Collins, handing him a red windbreaker. "It's getting a little chilly out."

Hawkeye slipped the jacket on over his blue-and-white striped rugby shirt, and then was out the door, a couple of big real estate books under each arm.

Mrs. Fields lived in the same neighborhood, just down Crestview Drive in a ranch-style house similar to Hawkeye's. Nosey, running about, followed Hawkeye and Mrs. Fields all the way there.

"Thanks so much, Hawkeye," said Mrs. Fields when they reached her house. She opened the front door with a key. "If you'll just put the books on the dining room table, that'd be terrific."

Mrs. Fields stepped into the house and hurried toward the dining room to turn on the lights.

"Stay, Nosey," said Hawkeye, on the doorstep. "I'll be right back."

Suddenly, he heard Mrs. Fields cry out. "Oh, no! My crystal candelabrum—oh, it's smashed!"

Leaving the front door open behind him, Hawkeye rushed into the house. A large, crystal candelabrum lay broken on the dining room table. Tiny pieces of shattered crystal covered the table and floor.

"Oh, how dreadful! It was my wedding present from my parents. And now it's absolutely ruined! How on earth did this happen?"

Just then, the back door slammed. Laurie, Mrs. Fields' teenaged daughter, called out from the kitchen.

"Hi, I'm home! Anyone here?"

"Laurie, come in here, quickly!" said Mrs. Fields, still staring in dismay at the ruined candelabrum.

"In a sec. Let me get my jacket off." Laurie came in a moment later, stopped suddenly, and in amazement said, "Oh, Mom, what happened?"

"The candelabrum. I don't know how this happened. I just got home, too." Mrs. Fields put her hand to her mouth. "You don't suppose someone broke in, do you? You don't think we've been robbed?"

The phone started to ring. Barking loudly, Nosey shot through the open front door, bounded past Mrs. Fields, and slid into the kitchen.

"Oh, dear!" cried Mrs. Fields as Nosey zoomed by.

"Nosey!" shouted Hawkeye. "Don't answer the phone! It's not ours!"

But it was too late. Nosey ran to the phone and tried to pick up the receiver in her mouth. She held it for a moment, but then dropped it. The phone fell to the floor. Hawkeye, close behind her, picked up the receiver, which Nosey was still reaching for with her mouth.

"Hello? Hello?" said Hawkeye into the phone. "Is anyone there?"

"Ow, my ear . . ."

"Uh-oh," said Hawkeye. "Mom?"

"Hawkeye, is that you?" said Mrs. Collins. "What did you do, drop the phone into the garbage disposal?"

"Um, I'll explain later. Mrs. Fields just found her crystal candleholder broken, and she's kind of upset."

"Well, maybe you'd better come home," said Mrs. Collins. "Listen, I called to tell Mrs. Fields that she left her purse here. Could you come back and get it for her?"

"Sure." Just then, Hawkeye noticed something odd. He paused. "Mom, I've got to go, okay? I'll be home real soon."

"Fine. Bye."

Laurie came into the kitchen, got a broom and dustpan, and went back into the dining room.

Hawkeye hung up the phone and picked up a nearby note pad and pencil. He had a

Maybe he'd be able to figure out how the crystal candelabrum had been broken.

great eye for details—that's how he had gotten his nickname, "Hawkeye"—and when something was out of place, he always noticed it. And right now, there was something that seemed suspicious.

Hawkeye automatically started to draw. He raised his head, squinted, and studied the scene, and then quickly sketched what he saw. Maybe, just maybe, his sketch would reveal a clue and he'd be able to figure out how Mrs. Fields' crystal candelabrum had been broken. As Hawkeye sketched, Nosey sat by his side.

"Not bad," he murmured when he finished, several minutes later.

As he studied the sketch, trying to solve the mystery, Laurie came into the kitchen with a dustpan full of broken crystal. All of a sudden, Hawkeye realized what was wrong.

"Laurie, you'd better look at this!" he exclaimed, pointing to his drawing.

WHAT DID HAWKEYE SEE THAT WAS WRONG?

The Case of the Chocolate Snatcher

Hawkeye and his friend Amy were visiting Sergeant Treadwell at the police station. They had met the sergeant a year ago at their school's career days, and had helped him on a number of cases since then. Suddenly, Molly, who worked at Townsend Drugs, burst into the office.

"Oh, Sergeant!" she screamed, throwing her arms up in the air. "Oh, like, totally the worst thing's happened—the drugstore's been robbed!"

Molly, who used to baby-sit for Hawkeye and Amy, had recently graduated from high school and was now studying to be an actress.

She had spent a year in California, and now was back in Lakewood Hills, clerking at her dad's drugstore.

Molly batted her eyes dramatically. "Oh, like wow, I think I'm gonna faint." She teetered back and forth.

Amy, as fast moving as she was fast thinking, jumped up. "Catch her, Sarge!"

Sergeant Treadwell, a peanut butter sandwich in one hand and a carton of milk in the other, flung his arms around Molly as she wilted in his direction. He spilled milk all over her pants and smeared peanut butter in her hair. Molly's eyes burst open in horror.

"Omigosh!" she screamed as she examined herself. "This is too gross!"

Sergeant Treadwell turned as red as the siren on top of his squad car. "I'm sorry, really I am." He threw aside his lunch and started searching for a paper towel.

"The drugstore was robbed?" asked Hawkeye, coming right to the point.

"When? What was taken?" asked Amy, poised to reach for Sergeant Treadwell's phone.

Molly ran her hands through her hair. "Oh, my hair, like, totally yuk, y'know? Totally." She squinched up her nose and turned to Hawkeye and Amy.

"Right," she said, as if she really didn't care about the robbery anymore. "Someone just ripped off all the Turtles and Truffles."

"The what?" asked Sergeant Treadwell.

"You know, like chocolates. Like, Turtles are pecans, caramel and milk chocolate," replied Molly. "They cost, like, twenty dollars a pound."

Amy interrupted. "Were you there?"

"Yeah."

Hawkeye checked the digital clock on his pen. "When did it happen?"

Molly shrugged. "I don't know. Like, just a few minutes ago."

"Was anyone hurt?" asked Amy impatiently. "Did the robber get away?"

"Sergeant, could you hurry up with that towel?" demanded Molly. "No. No one was hurt. But the guy got away with two whole trays of chocolates—almost two hundred dollars' worth. That really gags me. He dumped them into a shopping bag and took off."

Sergeant Treadwell finally found the paper towels and handed them to Molly. She grabbed them and started to wipe herself off, more concerned with the mess than with the robbery.

"It's, like, on my jeans and everything," she said, dabbing at the peanut butter and milk on her pants. "Awesome. They're my favorite jeans. Man, I hope they're not totaled."

11

Sergeant Treadwell took a deep breath, sucking the air deep into his lungs. "I'm really, really, really, really sorry. I'm really—"

Hawkeye cut him off. "Well, what did the robber look like?" He pulled out his pen and pad. "You must have gotten a good look at him."

"Oh, yeah," said Molly. "He had enormous eyes, no ears, and leathery skin. Like, he was wearing a Halloween mask and he looked like some creature from outer space. He pulled it off as he ran out the door—it's still back at the store."

"What about his car?" Frustrated that they weren't getting very far, Amy pulled at one of her red pigtails. "Did you notice anything?"

Shuffling through the papers on his desk, the sergeant said, "Good question, Amy. Did you notice anything about the car, Molly? Perhaps if we could find the car ..."

"Well," began Molly, "it was a big brown car. It had a white roof, I guess. And on the rear bumper, there was, like, a bumper sticker. I remember reading it as the car sped away. Now, what did it say? Oh, yeah. Something like, 'Love is ageless ...'"

Amy's face turned pale. "'... visit your grandparents today'?"

"Omigosh!" cried Molly. "That's exactly what the sticker said. 'Love is ageless—visit your grandparents today.'"

12

"Yes, but . . ." Horrified, Amy turned to Hawkeye. "Mr. Harrison has a sticker like that on *his* brown car."

Every fall Amy and her family went apple picking in Mr. Harrison's apple orchard. Every Christmas they got their tree from him.

"No," said Amy, shaking her head firmly. "It *couldn't* be him. Not Mr. Harrison. He wouldn't rob anyone."

"Still, I'd better check him out," said Sergeant Treadwell as he gathered his things. "After all, his car is the only lead I have."

"Hey, Sarge," said Hawkeye, shoving his pad back in his pocket, "can we go with you?"

"Sure. You and Amy can show me where this Mr. Harrison lives."

Hawkeye and Amy grabbed their backpacks. They followed Sergeant Treadwell out the door. Molly, however, stayed behind.

"Aren't you coming?" asked Hawkeye.

"Are you serious?" said Molly in disbelief. "Like, there's no way I'm going out in the street like this. I'm going to call my mother and tell her to come pick me up. I've got to, y'know, wash my hair and change my jeans."

Hawkeye and Amy looked at one another and rolled their eyes. They left Molly behind and followed Sergeant Treadwell to his squad car. They clambered into the back seat of the car.

"Hawkeye," said Amy, fidgeting with nervousness, "it couldn't have been Mr. Harrison. He's such a sweet man." She sighed. "Maybe I'm wrong. Maybe he doesn't really have a brown car, after all."

"Come on, Amy, let's do some figuring," said Hawkeye. He pulled out his pad and pen and started to sketch what had happened, based on Molly's story. "Let's just start from the beginning and work through the whole thing."

"Well," said Amy, "Townsend Drugs was robbed about a half-hour ago."

Hawkeye checked the clock on his pen. "That means that at about 3:30 a masked man robbed Townsend Drugs and all he took was some chocolates."

"That doesn't tell us much, does it?"

Amy frowned. "Nope. But we can't give up. Let's think."

They arrived at Mr. Harrison's farm a few minutes later. Mr. Harrison's car was there, backed into a small garage. It tilted to one side as if it had a flat tire.

A teenaged boy came out of the garden and walked towards them.

"That's Ted," explained Amy. "He works for Mr. Harrison."

Sergeant Treadwell opened his car door and got out. Hawkeye and Amy hesitated and then climbed out, too. While the sergeant talked, Hawkeye continued sketching and Amy scouted around.

"Hello, Sergeant," said Ted. "What can I do for you?"

"Well, there's been a drugstore robbery," said Sergeant Treadwell, embarrassed. "I was wondering if anyone around here might know anything about it."

"Robbery?" Ted scratched his head. "Why would we know anything about a robbery?"

"A car like Mr. Harrison's was seen in the area," said Sarge.

"Oh." Ted paused a moment. "Sorry, but I don't know anything about any robbery. I've been working in the garden all afternoon. Maybe you could ask Mr. Harrison or Tom, his nephew."

Just then Tom came around the side of the house.

"Hey, Tom," yelled Ted, "get your uncle. Sergeant Treadwell wants to ask him some questions about a robbery at Townsend Drugs."

"Sure," Tom yelled back.

A moment later he and his uncle stood in the yard talking to the sergeant.

"I've been out in the apple orchard all afternoon," Tom explained.

"And I've been sleeping," said Mr. Harrison. "I've got a bit of a cold."

He pulled out his pad and pen and started to sketch what had happened, based on Molly's story.

"Oh," said Sergeant Treadwell. "Well, as I was saying to Ted, a car like yours was seen near the robbery."

Mr. Harrison turned to the garage. Amy was there, inspecting the tire.

"This thing's as flat as a pancake," she said. "There's a big nail in it."

Mr. Harrison looked puzzled. "Now, I wonder when that happened," he said.

Ted came up. "No one could have gone far on that."

Sergeant Treadwell looked at the car and nodded. "You're right. I hadn't noticed that. Well, sorry to disturb you."

The sergeant turned and started for the squad car. Hawkeye finished the drawing he was doing and ran over to him.

"Psst, Sarge," said Hawkeye, "One of those guys is lying. Look at this!"

HOW DID HAWKEYE KNOW SOMEBODY WAS LYING?

The Mystery of Lucy's Revenge

"Lucy, you can't come with Hawkeye and me to the movies," said Amy to her younger sister. "You wouldn't understand it. You're too young."

Lucy stuck her tongue out in the space where she should have had two front teeth. "Phooey. I am not too young. I would too under*th*tand everything." Lucy scratched her blonde hair, then jammed her hands in the pocket of her overalls. "Mommy *thayth* I'm very mature. You know, I *th*tarted reading when I wa*th* three."

"Yeah, but Lucy, you're still only six. You still haven't got all your grownup teeth. And this is going to be a scary movie."

"I bet you guy*th* will get i*the* cream after it, too."

"No way," said Amy, slipping on a green sweater with her initials on the front. "I'm coming right home because I'm right in the middle of the greatest book. I have to finish it tonight, too, because it's due at the library tomorrow."

"Amy," whined Lucy, "you take me to the movie or I'll tell Mom you paid me a dollar to clean up your room."

Amy froze. She knew she'd be grounded for that. "Lucy, don't you dare! If you tell Mom that, I'll tell her that the reason you were sick last week was because you used that dollar to buy a tube of raw cookie dough. And then you ate the whole thing. That's why you were sick!"

Lucy was furious. "Oh, rat*th*!" she yelled as she stomped off.

Relieved that she wouldn't get caught for bribing Lucy, Amy brushed her shoulder-length red hair and put on her navy windbreaker. Then she went outside. Hawkeye was sitting on his bike, waiting for her.

"Lucy wanted to come, but I wouldn't let her," explained Amy. "She'd get too scared.

Then Mom and Dad would yell at me for taking her to such a scary movie in the first place."

Amy hopped on her bike. "What do you bet that Lucy pulls some kind of trick to get back at me? She always does that when she's mad."

Hawkeye grinned. "Your kid sister may be short on teeth, but she sure is long on ideas."

"Yeah, I'll say."

Amy and Hawkeye coasted behind the house and took the shortcut to the movie theater. Riding across the Mill Creek Bridge, they pedaled across the football field and behind Lakewood Hills Elementary. They arrived at the theater with just enough time to buy some popcorn and get good seats in the third row, their favorite spot.

The movie was full of the best special effects, and they both screamed a lot. When it was over, Hawkeye said, "Wow, I'm wiped out. I can't even move."

"Yeah, me too," replied Amy. "What a great movie."

"I liked the part about the monster coming out of the food processor."

"The part when they cloned the mean baby-sitter was the coolest," said Amy.

They biked home the long route. When they got back, Hawkeye saw some kids playing soccer.

"Want to play, Amy?" he asked.

"Nope. I'm reading this great book about pioneers," said Amy. "I have to finish tonight because it's due at the library tomorrow."

"Too bad," said Hawkeye, glancing at the soccer players. "Looks like they could've used your help. See you tomorrow."

"Bye."

Amy parked her bike in the garage and went in. As she took off her windbreaker, she looked around for her book. But the book wasn't on the table where she had left it.

"Ah, Lucy, now what?" she groaned when she spotted a folded note in its place. "Not another secret code."

Mumbling to herself, Amy went over and unfolded the message.

"Lucy!" yelled Amy as loudly as she could. She was so mad she didn't even move. "Lucy, darn you, where's my book? I have to finish it!"

But Lucy didn't answer. She was nowhere around.

"Oh, Lucy! You and your secret codes." Amy sighed and sat down. "If I want to finish that book, I guess the only thing I can do is try and figure this thing out."

She went over the message, letter by letter.

Amy read through the message and found nothing. On her second time through, though, she noticed something. She went over the message letter by letter.

"Aha!" she said, a moment later. Amy's frown turned into a smile. "I'm still smarter than my kid sister!"

WHERE DID LUCY HIDE AMY'S BOOK?

The Secret of the Almost Accident

One warm, sunny, fall afternoon, Hawkeye and Amy biked out to Clear Lake to join Sergeant Treadwell. He had been there since early morning, and had promised them that the fishing would be terrific.

But just as they pedaled over the top of a large hill, they heard an enormous, roaring crash from below. Seconds later, a car skidded to a halt.

"Look, Amy!" said Hawkeye, pointing down the hill. "A humungous load of lumber just fell off that truck into the middle of the road. That's pretty weird."

"Yeah, and now that sports car can't get through the intersection. Come on, let's go see."

Hawkeye and Amy raced down the hill. When they reached the intersection, Amy recognized the driver of the sports car.

"Hi, Dr. Ramirez. Remember me? I'm Amy Adams. You fixed my little sister Lucy's finger when she broke it. What happened?"

"Hi, Amy. That idiot truck driver spilled all this lumber right in the middle of the road. I could have been hurt! And since I can't get around it, I'll never make it to town in time for the auction."

The truck driver, a big, burly man wearing a "TMJ Supplies" t-shirt, came around the side of the truck. "Hey, mister, what am I supposed to do? I was just taking this load of lumber to the new housing development, Rosewood Homes. One of the ropes must have broken or something. It'll only take an hour or so to get this cleaned up."

"An hour!" cried Dr. Ramirez. He pounded his fist on the hood of his car. "I'm going to miss the auction. I'll never get the car of my dreams!"

The driver started to clear the intersection, board by board.

"I don't get it, Dr. Ramirez," said Hawkeye. "What's so special about an auction today?"

The doctor turned to Hawkeye. "Special? I'll tell you what's special. Scott Ray, the owner of the second Model T ever made, decided he wanted to sell it. Mr. Ray knew that Tom Johnson and I have been dying to buy his car for years. So he invited Johnson and me to an auction at his house today."

"You want to borrow my bike?" suggested Amy.

"Thanks, but it's much too far," said Dr. Ramirez. "I'd never make it in time."

"Well, we could bike to a phone and tell Mr. Ray that you're going to be a little late," said Hawkeye.

"Thank you. But I'm supposed to be there in five minutes." Dr. Ramirez sighed. "Mr. Ray said that if one of us didn't show up, he'd just sell it to the other. He made it perfectly clear that he wouldn't bother to wait."

"At least you weren't hurt," said Amy. "I mean, you could have run right into the truck—or the lumber could've crashed down on you."

"But this is worse! This is the absolute worst thing that could have happened!" The doctor turned red with anger.

Hawkeye nudged Amy and said quietly, "Let's leave him alone."

"I'm still going to bike to the lake and get Sarge," Amy said. She glanced over at the

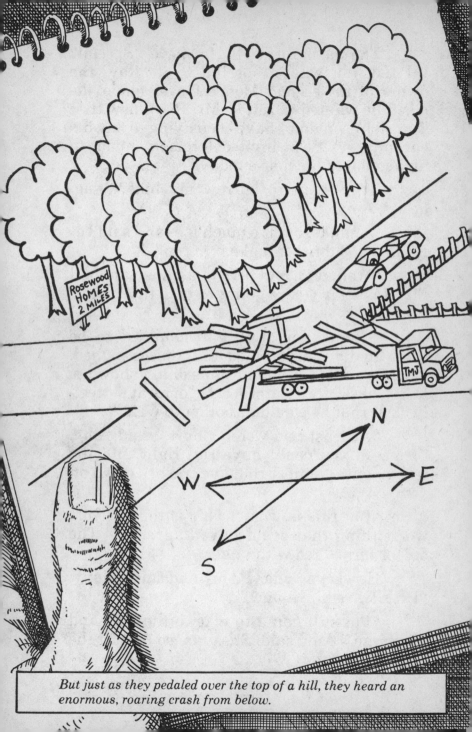

But just as they pedaled over the top of a hill, they heard an enormous, roaring crash from below.

doctor and shook her head. "I can't imagine getting that upset about a silly old car."

"Well, a Model T is a pretty neat car." Hawkeye laughed. "You're right, though, it's sort of silly. Anyway, I'll wait here for you and Sarge. I think I'll take a look around. There are a few things I want to check out."

Hawkeye walked all the way around the truck. He watched as the driver slowly picked up the lumber. Then he hurried up the side of the hill so that he could get a good perspective on the entire accident. Yes, he could see that something was definitely wrong.

Hawkeye wiped his glasses, then pulled out his sketch pad and pencil and started to draw at once. He carefully drew in the intersection, the truck, the car, and the pile of lumber.

"Just as I thought," he said to himself, scratching his elbow.

Just then, Sergeant Treadwell pulled up in his squad car with Amy seated next to him.

"Hey, Sarge!" shouted Hawkeye, running down the hill and waving his drawing in the air. "Radio headquarters! Tell them to call Mr. Ray and warn him not to sell his Model T to Mr. Johnson! I've figured out the scheme!"

WHAT SCHEME DID HAWKEYE DISCOVER?

The Case of Double Trouble

Hawkeye thought he'd go cross-eyed if he had to look at his math book a second longer. So when the upstairs phone rang, he jumped up. Ever since his teacher, Mr. Bronson, had told his parents that he could do much better at math, he'd had to study it a half-hour longer every day after school.

"Whew, saved by the bell." He charged out of his bedroom and into the hall.

"No, Nosey, I got it!" he shouted, trying to beat his dog to the phone. "You're not supposed to do that trick anymore."

He picked up the phone on the second ring. "Hello?"

As if she had been cheated out of her fun, Nosey put her tail between her legs and slunk off.

"Hawkeye? Is that you?" said a frightened boy's voice.

"Yeah, who's this?"

"It's Buffy. You've got to come over quick! Grandpa's hurt!"

Buffy and Duffy were eight-year-old, identical twins. They often stayed with their grandfather, who lived only two doors down from Hawkeye on Crestview Drive.

"Buffy," said Hawkeye, clutching the phone tightly in his hands, "what is it? What happened?"

"Oh, Hawkeye, we're scared! Grandpa's on the floor, and he can't wake up!"

"I'll get Dad and we'll be right there!"

Hawkeye and his father reached the neighboring house in a few minutes. Shaking with fear, Buffy led the way to his grandfather, who was lying on his back in the bedroom hall. Duffy was by his grandfather's side. The old man was now awake and struggling to sit up.

"Wait just a minute. You don't want to strain yourself," said Mr. Collins. He examined the hurt man. "That's a nasty bump you've got on the back of your head."

Grandpa opened his eyes and blinked. "Ew, maheh," he mumbled.

"What did he say, Dad?" asked Hawkeye.

"I don't know. I couldn't understand him, either." Mr. Collins asked, "Are you all right? What happened?"

Grandpa blinked his eyes. "Ew, maheh. Ah shwip ondadurn wawabawoom." He sounded as if he had a mouthful of marbles.

"I still don't understand, but that's okay," said Mr. Collins to the older man. "Just relax. I think we better get you to a doctor and have you checked out. Hawkeye, you stay here with the twins while we go to the doctor."

He hurried home and returned in his car. With Mr. Collins on one side and Hawkeye on the other, they helped the grandfather out of the house. The twins calmed down, relieved to see that their grandfather was in good hands.

"He'll be okay, won't he, Hawkeye?" asked Duffy, as Mr. Collins drove off with their grandfather.

"Oh, sure. But what happened?"

The twins looked at one another and said nothing.

Finally, Buffy spoke. "It's a mystery." He glanced at his brother.

"Yeah, a real mystery," added Duffy. "Maybe you can figure it out."

"Well, you gotta tell me everything that happened," said Hawkeye suspiciously. He knew that the twins often got into trouble.

Once they had sneaked into the dog pound and accidentally opened the electric gates, letting all the dogs out. It had taken three days to round them all up.

"I can't solve a case unless you tell me everything," Hawkeye told them sternly. *"Everything."*

Buffy pointed down the hall and into the kitchen. There was an open bag of Nutty Nut cookies on the table, along with some empty milk glasses.

"We were all sitting in there having a snack," he said.

"Right," said Duffy.

"Then there was this noise," Buffy continued. "A big noise from the bedroom."

"Right. And it scared Buffy and me." Duffy's eyes were big with excitement. "But it didn't scare Grandpa. Nope, not him. He just got up and went to see what it was."

"Yeah, and he went down the hall. There was another big noise. But Grandpa wasn't scared at all."

Hawkeye already doubted that the twins were telling him the truth.

"You mean, the noise came from back there?" asked Hawkeye, trying to get to the bottom of things.

"Yep," said Buffy. He pushed open the door to his grandfather's bedroom. "Grandpa came back here and opened the door and then—"

"Then," said Duffy, cutting in, "two big robbers hit Grandpa over the head!"

"Yeah, that's what happened! Grandpa came back here, opened the door, and discovered them. They came in through the bedroom window while we were having cookies and milk. And then the two robbers escaped out the window!"

The twins looked at each other for a second and then turned back to Hawkeye.

"Well," said Duffy, firmly, "that's what happened. Can you help us find the robbers or should we call Sergeant Treadwell or something?"

Hawkeye quietly said to himself, "Oh, brother."

He reached into his back pocket and took out his sketch pad and pencil, confident that if he sketched the area he'd be able to find out what really had happened.

Noting every detail, Hawkeye paced this way and that. He walked up and down the hallway, examined the floor for any clues, and finally zeroed in on the bedroom. The twins, right on Hawkeye's heels, were impressed by his seriousness.

"Hey," said Hawkeye, nudging Buffy and Duffy backward, "give a man room to sketch."

"*I know who the real criminals are and just what really happened to your grandpa,*" *Hawkeye said.*

They giggled and whispered back and forth. Five minutes later, Hawkeye showed them his drawing.

He said, "I know who the real criminals are and just what really happened to your grandpa."

Buffy and Duffy, their mouths wide open, were speechless.

WHAT REALLY HAPPENED TO GRANDPA?

The Mystery of the Crook Convention

Hawkeye and Amy sat amid an assortment of fishing tropies in Sergeant Treadwell's office and watched as the sergeant poured hot fudge over three dishes of ice cream. As always, an ice cream party was a signal that Sergeant Treadwell had a case he couldn't solve.

"Hey, that's enough," said Hawkeye. "You don't want me to overdose on hot fudge, do you? I mean, I want to be able to find the ice cream underneath."

"Sarge," said Amy, waving her hands, "that's plenty for me, too. I can always eat a lot more hot fudge than broccoli, but I know my limits. And half a jar of hot fudge is max."

Sergeant Treadwell set the nearly empty jar next to his wife's photo and licked his fingers. "Well, there's supposed to be some sort of gathering of crooks tomorrow and I need your help to find out where they're meeting. I just want to make sure you've got everything you need to help you think well."

Hawkeye grinned. "In that case, how about a little whipped cream and one of those red cherries?"

"You got it." The rather pudgy sergeant picked up a can of whipped cream and shook it. "Believe me, these are going to be terrific sundaes."

Sergeant Treadwell squirted a big mound of whipped cream onto the ice cream. Then he shoved his hand into a jar of cherries. Hawkeye, squinting out of one eye, was certain that the sergeant's hand would be too chubby for the jar. And it was.

"Oops," said the sergeant, trying to yank his hand out of the jar. "I got my hand *in* there, but, but . . ."

Hawkeye saw it coming and winced. The sergeant's hand suddenly popped out of the jar and he lost his balance. Teetering backwards, he upset a wastepaper basket full of crumpled paper.

"Oh, oh, oh!"

Amy leaped up. "Careful!"

With one hand she steadied the sergeant, and with one foot she caught the wastepaper basket before its contents had completely spilled out.

"Bravo!" said Hawkeye, clapping his hands above his head.

"Yes, well, um, thanks, Amy," said Sergeant Treadwell sheepishly.

Trying to be a little more cautious, he put a couple of cherries on top of each sundae, and passed them to Hawkeye and Amy. After a minute of silence and several big bites, they got down to business.

"Okay, here's the deal," said Sergeant Treadwell. "I've heard rumors of some sort of meeting of crooks tomorrow. You know, kind of a crooks' convention. Well, I had one guy in for questioning on a robbery, and I asked him about this meeting. The guy said he didn't know anything, but I found this piece of paper on the floor after he had left. It's written in some kind of code—I think it has to do with the meeting tomorrow."

Sergeant Treadwell put his sundae to the side and laid a strip of paper on the table before him. Hawkeye and Amy leaned forward and examined it.

"That's something, all right," said Amy, wiping her mouth with the back of her hand. "But I'm not sure what."

41

The sergeant shook his head. "I've been looking and looking at it, but I just can't make sense of it. The only thing I can figure is that something is happening at noon and a woman named Eva might be there. But without her last name, I'm lost. I just can't break the code."

He handed the piece of paper to Hawkeye and Amy. "Here, you see if you two can figure it out."

As Sergeant Treadwell passed the paper to Amy, it slipped out of his hand. It fell to the floor and landed with the message facing him.

"I'll get it, Sarge," said Amy, reaching for the paper. She paused for a moment and studied the paper as it lay on the floor.

"Hmm . . . sometimes . . . sometimes you just have to look at things differently," she muttered.

"What are you getting at?" asked Hawkeye.

Amy snapped her fingers and grabbed the piece of paper. "Come on, guys, you just have to be creative."

Sergeant Treadwell threw up his hands. "Amy, will you tell me what's going on? Have you broken the code or haven't you?"

Amy handed the message to Hawkeye, and sat back and stirred her ice cream and hot fudge into brown mush. "Oh, I've figured it out, all right," she said, laughing. "But you

noon teem

b1 tp a

eva eniam 88

"The guy said he didn't know anything, but I found this piece of paper on the floor," Sarge said.

might have to give me another sundae to get me to talk."

WHERE WAS THE CROOK CONVENTION GOING TO BE HELD?

The Mystery of the Disk Swiper

Amy came running full speed into the library.

"Hawkeye! Hawkeye!" she yelled. "You won't believe it. The worst. The absolute worst. Man, oh, man, oh, man. Why us?"

"Amy, what is it?" asked Hawkeye. "What happened?"

"The video game disk—the one we've spent weeks working on in the computer club—is gone." Amy and Hawkeye both belonged to the Bytes of Data Computer Club.

"They took both copies, too," Amy added. She shook her head. "It's the pits.

45

Today was supposed to be the first day the other kids could come in after school to play it."

"Oh, no. What a bummer." Hawkeye slapped his forehead. "I already began collecting money from the kids who wanted to play it this afternoon."

"Hawkeye and Amy," called the attractive, young librarian. "Can I help you? Just yoo-hoo."

Amy signaled Hawkeye to follow her. The two of them left the library and headed for the computer room.

"Any clues, any idea who might have stolen the game?" asked Hawkeye as they walked down the hall.

"Not really, but I think it might have been some kids from the high school," said Amy. "What creeps! They visited the computer room last week and really liked the game. They asked and asked for a copy of it, but we wouldn't give it to them. I suppose the only thing we can do now is use the game Randy made up at home."

"I guess so," said Hawkeye. "I mean, it's an okay game and everything, but it would have been neater to use the one we all worked on."

Just as they neared the computer room, Randy, a pudgy, shy boy who was in the computer club, too, came trotting toward them.

"Hey, Hawkeye! Amy!" he shouted, waving an envelope and a piece of paper in one hand. "I was standing by the front door and some big guy shoved this envelope in my hand. He said it was for the computer club."

"Was it one of the high school kids?" asked Amy immediately.

"Um, I think so."

Amy nudged Hawkeye. "I told you. It was those high school kids. They're trying to get back at us because we wouldn't give them the game."

"I think that's it," said Randy, pushing his glasses up on his nose. "I opened the envelope and read it. This is terrible."

"I'll say," said Amy, shaking her head. "Oh, brother."

Hawkeye said, "Hey, Randy. We already collected money from the kids who wanted to play our game this afternoon. But since it's been stolen, do you think we could use your game instead?"

Randy blinked in surprise. "Oh, sure. I suppose you could. From the letter, it looks like we won't be getting ours back for a while."

Randy handed the envelope and letter to Amy. She and Hawkeye read through it several times. Suddenly, Amy's eyes grew big. She took the letter and gave Hawkeye a shove toward the computer room.

Dear Bytes of Data Computer Club,

We have your silly video game and we'll return it if and when we feel like it. It's really a pretty silly game after all. We'll let you know when we've decided.

The Digital Thieves

"I was standing by the front door and some big guy shoved this envelope in my hand," Randy said.

"Hawkeye," she said, "don't say anything. I know how to get the game back. I don't have time to explain, but Randy and I can handle it."

Hawkeye was confused. "Amy, what are you talking about?"

"Don't worry. We'll be right there. This is my mystery and I've already solved it."

Amy turned and quickly headed down the hall. Randy hurried after her.

HOW WAS AMY ABLE TO FIND THE VIDEO GAME DISK?

The Case of the Stolen Samovar

Pushing ahead as they climbed the stairs to the apartment in downtown Lakewood Hills, Amy said to Hawkeye, "Aunt Olga's not really my aunt, but she's just like one. She's my grandmother's best friend."

"When was her apartment robbed?" asked Hawkeye.

"Just this morning. Oh, and Hawkeye, Aunt Olga has a strong Russian accent. She was born in Russia—and just about everyone else in this building was, too."

They reached the apartment and were greeted by Aunt Olga, a blonde, older woman wearing a blue dress.

"Amy, Hawkeye, my darlin*k*s," said Aunt Olga in her thick accent, after Amy introduced Hawkeye. "You must to come in and see *v*hat a mess there is."

They entered the apartment and did indeed find a mess. A chair was tipped over, some drawers were open, and a box of sewing things was spilled on the floor. Beneath a window were a foreign newspaper and a monogrammed handkerchief.

"Wow," said Hawkeye under his breath to Amy, "this is worse than my room."

"Mine, too," Amy whispered back.

"This is terrible, no?" said Aunt Olga. "I *v*as goin*k* to the store, and all *v*as good. But *v*hen I come to home, such a disaster. The burglar must to have heard me comin*k*. He flew out the *v*indow and down the fire escape."

"Has Sergeant Treadwell been here yet?" asked Amy.

"Da, da, da," said Aunt Olga in Russian, meaning yes. "He *v*as here. But, Amy, your grandmother says you and Hawkeye very, very good at this. She said you *v*ere such good sl . . . sl . . ." Aunt Olga put her hand to her chin and tried to remember. "How do you call that word?"

"Sleuths?" suggested Hawkeye.

"Da, that's it," said Aunt Olga, snapping her fingers. "So, you are pretty good sleuths, yes?"

"Well, we try pretty hard," said Amy. She added eagerly, "And I hope we'll solve this case, too."

"I'll say," said Hawkeye as he pulled out his sketch pad and pencil. "Did the thief get away with anything?"

Aunt Olga became very sad. "Oh, yes. Vhen I come to America, my parents brink a samovar."

"What's a samovar?" asked Amy.

"How to explain? Vell, it is a large device for makink tea. And my family brought very, very old and very, very beautiful brass samovar from Russia." Aunt Olga wiped her eyes. "This is vhat the thief stole from me. My samovar."

"Do you have any idea who might have taken it?" asked Hawkeye.

Aunt Olga wiped her eyes. "Vell, if you ask me, I think it vas someone in the buildink. You must to know that everyone in this buildink is from Russia. And everyone *loves* my samovar. The downstairs doors are locked, too, so it vould have been big trouble for stranger to come in."

"What about any clues?" asked Amy. "Did you find anything?"

"Oh, sure." Aunt Olga pointed to a monogrammed handkerchief on the floor. "There is that and that Russian newspaper, too. They must to have fallen out of the thief's pocket *v*hen he flew out the *v*indow."

Hawkeye stepped closer to the newspaper, which lay on the floor. "You mean all of this is in Russian?"

"Sure. From New York. It's called *Russkoye Slovo*. That's *v*hat it says at the top of the paper. It means 'The Russian Word.' "

"Boy, the Russian alphabet sure is different from ours," said Amy. "It must take an age and a half to learn."

Aunt Olga laughed. "No, darlin*k*. It's not very hard at all. Some Russian letters are even like English ones. For example, the Russian 'o' is also the English 'o.' Of course, some are totally different. For instance, the English 'p' is the Russian 'r.' "

A thought struck Amy. "Aunt Olga, do you know everyone else who lives in the building?"

"Da, da, da." She thought for a moment. "There's Yuri Zhiguli, Leonid Chaika, Catherine Kofye, Serge Romanov, and Tanya Partiya."

Hawkeye wrote this down and said, "If we could only figure out who the handkerchief belongs to . . ."

He quickly started to draw Aunt Olga's apartment. He paused for a moment.

"My, vhat a quick drawer you are," said Aunt Olga, admiring the picture.

"Don't forget the newspaper," said Amy. "That's important. Maybe we can find out who that belongs to."

"Yep."

He was finished several minutes later.

"My, vhat a quick drawer you are," said Aunt Olga as she admired the picture. "This is vonderful."

A thought struck Hawkeye. "Wow." He slapped his forehead. "Of course!"

"Okay, Hawkeye," said Amy. "Out with it."

Hawkeye turned to Aunt Olga, a broad grin on his face. "I know who broke into your apartment!"

WHO BROKE INTO AUNT OLGA'S APART-MENT AND STOLE HER SAMOVAR?

THE SECRET OF THE
ANCIENT
TREASURE
THE SECRET ROOM
PART 2

What Happened in Volume 1

When Hawkeye and Amy were looking for fossils in a cave along Mill Creek, they discovered an old metal box buried deep in one of the underground rooms. Inside the box was a yellowed, frayed map, which clearly led to the von Buttermore estate. On the map were some mysterious letters and numbers written in code. At the end of "The Black Cave" (Part 1 of "The Secret of the Ancient Treasure"), Amy had just broken the code.

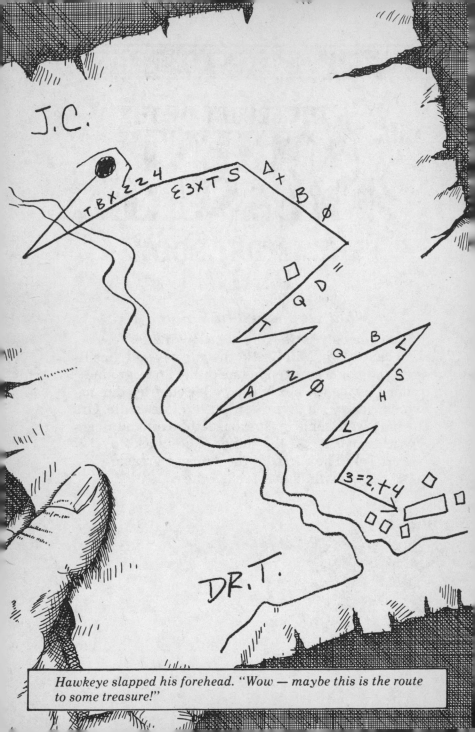

Hawkeye slapped his forehead. "Wow — maybe this is the route to some treasure!"

The Secret Room

Hawkeye had to know. "Amy, what do you mean, you broke the code? Come on, tell me what you found!"

"Look." She bent over the map, which was spread out on a boulder in front of the cave. "I saw something like this in Lucy's book of codes. The zigzag arrow doesn't lead anywhere except to the von Buttermore place. But there's a message buried in each corner and angle."

Hawkeye put a finger here and there on the map. "You mean . . . S . . . T . . . A . . . Hey," he said, excited, "there *is* something hidden here!"

Amy continued reading the message. "'L ... L ... 3.'" She stopped. That was the message. "Stall 3! They must be talking about something hidden in Stall 3—in the old stable."

"Amy, I bet you're right!" Hawkeye jumped up and began to fold the map. "Come on, let's go over and see Mrs. von Buttermore!"

They hurriedly gathered their things, then hopped on their borrowed dirt bikes and took off. Nosey, glad to be off on another adventure, loped ahead.

Within half an hour, they arrived at the von Buttermore mansion. They parked their bikes out front and left Nosey guarding them. Then the butler led them through hall after hall until they reached the drawing room. Mrs. von Buttermore, wearing a shimmering sari from India, rose to greet them.

"Why, Hawkeye and Amy," she said, extending her hand. "What a pleasant surprise."

Priceless, the black and white Great Dane, didn't even get to his feet, but lazily wagged his tail.

Amy couldn't hold back the news a moment longer. "Mrs. von Buttermore, you won't believe this! Hawkeye and I were in one of the Mill Creek caves—we heard there were lots of fossils there—and we walked way far in and found an underground river. And then, we found an old map buried in this box."

"Yeah. And the map leads here," Hawkeye added quickly. "And it says—we think, anyway—that there's something, treasure, maybe, hidden in Stall 3. You know, in the old stable."

"Now, slow down a minute," Mrs. von Buttermore said graciously. "Not so fast. I didn't get all of that."

Hawkeye and Amy slowly repeated their story. When they had told her everything, Mrs. von Buttermore asked, "So that's the box? May I see the map?"

"Sure." Amy reached over and worked the box cover loose, then took the map out.

"Over here. Bring it over here," said Mrs. von Buttermore. Her colorful dress swishing softly, she walked across the large room to a table and switched on a lamp.

"Now, let's take a look at this map," she said, patting the table. She took out a pair of bifocals and slipped them on.

Together, Hawkeye and Amy carefully spread the map out on the table, where the light beamed directly down on it. The moment Mrs. von Buttermore saw it, she cried out.

"Oh, my word!" She put her hand to her chest. "It's signed by Dr. T.!"

Hawkeye asked, "Who's Dr. T.?"

"This is incredible," said Mrs. von Buttermore softly to herself, her eyes widening. She addressed Hawkeye and Amy. "He was my grandfather's personal physician. His full name was Dr. Thomas, but everyone called him Dr. T. And he was a thief. A terrible thief."

"What did he steal?" asked Amy.

Mrs. von Buttermore took off her glasses and chewed thoughtfully on one of the stems. "My grandfather had a collection of ancient Egyptian gems and small gold statuettes," she said. "Dr. T. stole the entire collection right out from under his nose."

"Wow." Hawkeye thought this was the best story he'd heard in a long time. And it had really happened. "How'd he do it?"

"Grandpapa kept the collection locked up in his library," said Mrs. von Buttermore. "About eighty years ago, he decided to have some work done on this house—in here, in the drawing room, I believe. Anyway, Grandpapa became so frustrated trying to explain to a carpenter what he wanted done, that he tried to do it himself. He climbed up on a ladder and fell off."

"That's terrible," said Amy. "What happened? Was he okay?"

"Eventually. But Dr. T. ordered him to stay in bed for three weeks."

Hawkeye was spellbound. "And what then?"

"Well," said Mrs. von Buttermore, "he stayed in bed for two whole weeks. Then one night, he heard a noise from the library. He got up, hobbled in, and found Dr. T. stealing the last of the Egyptian statues. Grandpapa grabbed an antique sword, called the servants, and they came and chased Dr. T. right out of town."

"Did he get away?" Amy couldn't believe it. "With the statue, too?"

"Yes, but as far as anyone knew, only with that one. It turned out that all of the other Egyptian gems and statuettes were missing, too. No one ever found them. Everyone figured that Dr. T. had been stealing the Egyptian items one by one."

Suddenly Hawkeye remembered something from the map. He leaned over the table.

"'J.C.,'" he said. "Do those letters mean anything to you?"

Mrs. von Buttermore's eyes narrowed as she thought for a moment, staring at the letters.

"'J.C.' ... Of course. They could stand for Jesse Carter, the famous crook. The night the servants chased Dr. T. out of town, they learned that Jesse Carter was in the area. They suspected that he might somehow be connected with Dr. T., but nothing was ever proven. The sheriff did arrest Jesse Carter for an earlier bank robbery, though. Sent him to jail, too."

Amy thought out loud. "It looks like they really were working together—the map proves it. And I bet—"

"I bet we'll find the evidence in Stall 3," said Hawkeye, standing up.

"Well, what are we waiting for?" Mrs. von Buttermore grabbed a fold of her sari and started off. "Come on, let's go!"

The three of them dashed out of the drawing room and raced down the halls, past astonished servants, and out a side door. Not stopping for a moment, they cut across the wide lawn toward the old stable, an enormous structure of rock and wood. Hawkeye and Amy both helped Mrs. von Buttermore swing open the thick, heavy door.

"I haven't been here in years," said Mrs. von Buttermore, panting slightly. She tried a light switch, but it didn't work. "Oh, I forgot. The power line to the stable was cut during last year's ice storm. Since we don't use the building at all, I never got it repaired."

"I've still got my flashlight," said Hawkeye, pulling it out and flicking it on.

"Oh, good." Mrs. von Buttermore motioned into the dark stable. "Stall 3 is down there on the left."

The stable was dark, musty and cool. Thick ropes of cobwebs waved in every corner and the faint scent of long-gone horses lingered in the air. Amy, the fastest of the three, was out ahead. Mrs. von Buttermore followed her.

"This isn't what I would call the friendliest place," Amy said.

Hawkeye spotted a closed door off the stable's main aisle and swung it wide open. He aimed the flashlight into the room and recoiled in horror as Mrs. von Buttermore cried out.

"Stop, Hawkeye! Not that door!"

But it was too late. Inside the room, a dozen human skeletons hung like clothes in a gruesome closet.

"No!" Hawkeye cried, and slammed the door. "No!"

"Hawkeye!" shouted Amy, running to his side.

"Oh, dear, I forgot to warn you," said Mrs. von Buttermore, shaken up a bit herself. "Hawkeye, dear, I'm so sorry. Daddy always liked bones and he was forever studying anatomy as a hobby. They're not real skeletons, either. They're actually plaster. All of them. The university was getting rid of them and Daddy got a truckload deal—he couldn't pass it up."

Hawkeye took a deep breath and pushed his glasses up the bridge of his nose. "At this rate, I'm gonna be middle-aged by tomorrow morning."

Amy patted him on the shoulder. "Are you all right? You can put this one in your memoirs."

Hawkeye nodded and started off. "Hey, let's not forget Stall 3!"

"Hey, I see something and I bet you it's the clue we're looking for!" said Hawkeye.

They hurried down the aisle to the deserted stall.

"Do you see anything?" Hawkeye asked.

"No," said Mrs. von Buttermore.

Amy said, "Look for a false wall or a hiding place of some sort."

"If you two don't mind, I'm going to sit down," said Hawkeye, seating himself on a bale of hay. "You guys search and I'll do a drawing. Maybe the three of us working together can turn up something."

Amy and Mrs. von Buttermore began to go over the entire stall. While the older woman ran her fingers over the wall, Amy cleared away the straw and checked the floor in one corner. Mrs. von Buttermore checked the manger, an old bucket, and an old box. Amy started tapping on the wooden floor with her foot.

Meanwhile, Hawkeye sketched the outlines of Stall 3. As he filled in the details, he noticed something strangely out of place.

"Hey, I see something!" he said, standing up. "I see something and I bet you it's the clue we're looking for!"

WHAT IS THE CLUE IN HAWKEYE'S DRAWING?

For the solution to this story and more of "The Secret of the Ancient Treasure," see The Case of the Video Game Smugglers, *Volume 3 in the* **Can You Solve the Mystery?**™*series.*

SOLUTIONS

The Case of the Crashing Candelabrum

When he examined the things Laurie had brought home from school, Hawkeye saw something suspicious. From the order in which she had piled them on the chair, he could tell a little about what time she had returned home.

Hawkeye said, "Laurie, I don't know exactly when you got home, but I do know you've been here for awhile. If you had just walked in the door, your purse would have been at the bottom of the pile on the chair, and your book bag, jacket, and sweater would have been on top."

Laurie hesitated, and then confessed. "I got an 'A' on my French test, and I was so excited that I came running in to tell Mom. I came in through the front door and ran into the dining room, but then I tripped and bumped into the dinner table. The candelabrum wobbled back and forth, and then tipped over and smashed.

71

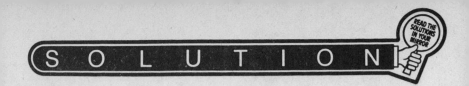
"I was so upset, Hawkeye, I just took off my backpack and coat and stuff and sat there. When I saw Mom coming up the sidewalk, I panicked. I locked the front door, put my things in the kitchen, and pretended I had just come home."

Laurie thought for a moment, and finally went in to tell her mother the truth. And her mother was mad—mad that Laurie hadn't told her the truth from the start.

The Case of the Chocolate Snatcher

Hawkeye wanted to show Sergeant Treadwell the sketch because it showed not one, but two drugstores.

"No one said which of the two drugstores had been robbed," said Hawkeye. "But Ted knew it was Townsend Drugs."

Amy came up. "That puncture mark in the tire is sort of strange. It looks like someone did it on purpose. And if that's so, someone could have used the car even this afternoon and then just let the air out of the tire."

When Sergeant Treadwell decided to ask Ted to come down to the police station to answer some more questions, Ted confessed. "I just had this irresistible urge for Turtles and Truffles and I was broke," he said.

Hawkeye, Amy, and the sergeant found what was left of the chocolates in the trunk of the car. When they returned them to Molly, she screamed, "Like, wow!" and gave them each a pound of Turtles. Ted worked nights at Townsend Drugs until he had earned enough money to pay for the chocolates he had stolen.

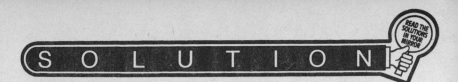

SOLUTION

READ THE SOLUTIONS IN YOUR MIRROR

The Mystery of Lucy's Revenge

Lucy had carefully arranged the words on the paper so that important letters landed on the lines formed by the creases.

"And if you read down the two creases," said Amy to herself, "you can read Lucy's coded message. She wrote, 'under my bed.' I bet the book is there."

Amy raced upstairs and found her book under Lucy's bed—and Lucy, too, flat on her stomach.

"What took you tho long, thmarty?" asked Lucy, as she handed Amy the book and crawled out.

"Well," Amy retorted, "if you could write better it would only have taken about half as long!"

SOLUTION

The Secret of the Almost Accident

Hawkeye realized that the truck, loaded with building supplies, was headed east, not west toward the new housing development. When Hawkeye remembered the initials on the driver's t-shirt, he realized whom the truck belonged to.

"I bet anything," he said, "that that truck belongs to Mr. Johnson—the owner of Tom M. Johnson Supply Company."

After hearing this, Sergeant Treadwell examined the ropes on the truck and found that they had been cut. The driver confessed that Mr. Johnson had sent him to block the road and prevent Dr. Ramirez from getting to the auction.

"Hey," said Dr. Ramirez, impressed, "you do have the eyes of a hawk, don't you, Hawkeye?"

Mr. Ray thought that anyone who would do what Mr. Johnson had done to get a car would not be a good owner of such a valuable classic, so he sold the Model T to Dr. Ramirez. The next week, the doctor took Hawkeye, Amy, and Sergeant Treadwell for a ride in his "new" jalopy.

79

The Case of Double Trouble

What really happened was that there were no burglars. First of all, the bedroom window was locked from the inside. Second, Grandpa was probably taking a nap: his bed was wrinkled and his false teeth were in a glass of water.

"Your grandfather couldn't have been eating nutty cookies because he didn't have his false teeth in. And there are only two milk glasses on the kitchen table," said Hawkeye. "But he was taking a nap later on, when you two started playing catch with a water balloon in the hall. I can see the broken balloon and the puddles of water."

The twins admitted that when the balloon broke, their grandfather woke up and was so annoyed that he got up without putting in his teeth. He came into the hall, slipped on the water, and hit his head.

Luckily, their grandfather's injury wasn't serious. And the twins were so sorry for what they had done that they were good for a whole week! Unfortunately for Hawkeye, that meant that they followed him everywhere, trying to learn how to be sleuths.

SOLUTION

The Mystery of the Crook Convention

"The crook convention's going to be held at this address," said Amy, pointing to the coded message.

When the piece of paper fell to the floor, Amy read it just as it was, even though the letters were upside down. The first thing she noticed was the number "88" and that it read the same both forwards and backwards. After she picked up the note, Amy started reading the message backwards, starting from the number "88."

Amy smiled. "Just read the whole thing backwards and it says: '88 maine ave apt 1b meet noon.'"

Beaming, Sergeant Treadwell took a big bite of ice cream. "Now, what would I do without you two?"

The Mystery of the Disk Swiper

Amy was able to find the video game simply by examining the ransom note and the envelope that Randy had said it had come in.

When she looked at the envelope, Amy remembered that the letter had been folded in half. Yet to fit inside the envelope, the letter would have had to be folded several times. Randy had clearly said, however, that he had opened the envelope and taken the letter out. Amy took Randy down the hall and asked him about this.

"Oh . . . oh, all right," said Randy, flushing with embarrassment. "I took the video game. I was going to give it back later. Honest. And I'm sorry. It's just that I thought the kids might like me more or something if they played my video game."

Amy promised Randy that she wouldn't tell anyone, and together they returned the video game disk to the club. Later, Amy asked Randy to go with her and some other kids to a movie that night.

The Case of the Stolen Samovar

The person who broke into Aunt Olga's apartment was indeed someone from her building.

Aunt Olga had said that the name of the newspaper, spelled Pycckoe Слово, was pronounced "Russkoye Slovo." Remembering that Aunt Olga had said our "p" was their "r," Hawkeye realized that our "c" was the Russian "s," based on the way she pronounced the name.

"I get it," said Amy, "The initials on the handkerchief aren't English letters—they're Russian ones."

"Right," said Hawkeye. "That means they don't stand for a name like 'Charles Potter,' but for a Russian name with the initials 'S.R.'"

Aunt Olga gasped. "Of course. It was Serge Romanov who took my samovar! I should have known."

They hurried downstairs and found Serge Romanov making a big batch of tea in the samovar. He said he had only borrowed it for the afternoon because he was homesick and it reminded him of his childhood.

Aunt Olga yelled at him, but her
anger quickly passed, and she, Hawkeye,
and Amy joined Serge for a cup of tea.

Readers' Survey

To the reader:

We'd like you to give us your opinions about this book to help us plan other mystery books. After you've read this book, please find a sheet of paper. Then answer the questions you see below on your sheet (be sure to number your answers). Please **don't** write in the book. Mail your answer sheet to:

Meadowbrook Press
Dept. CYSI-4
18318 Minnetonka Blvd.
Deephaven, MN 55391

Thanks a lot for your replies — they really help us!

1. What is the volume number on this book? (Look on the front cover.)

2. Where did you get this book? (Read all of the answers first. Then choose the one that is your choice and write the letter on your sheet.)

   2A. Gift
   2B. Bookstore
   2C. Other store
   2D. School library
   2E. Public library
   2F. Borrowed from a friend
   2G. Other (What?)

3. If you chose the book yourself, why did you choose it? (Be sure to read all of the answers listed first. Then choose the one that you like best and write the letter on your sheet.)

   3A. I like to read mysteries.
   3B. The cover looked interesting.
   3C. The title sounded good.
   3D. I like to solve mysteries.
   3E. A librarian suggested it.
   3F. A teacher suggested it.
   3G. A friend liked it.
   3H. The picture clues looked interesting.
   3I. Hawkeye and Amy looked interesting.
   3J. Other (What?)

4. How did you like the book? (Write your number choice on your sheet.)

   4A. Liked a lot   4B. Liked   4C. Not sure   4D. Didn't like

5. How did you like the picture clues? (Write your number choice on your sheet.)

   4A. Liked a lot   4B. Liked   4C. Not sure   4D. Didn't like

6. What story did you like best? Why?

7. What story did you like least? Why?

8. If you could change this book in any way, what would you do?

9. Would you like to read more stories about Hawkeye and Amy?

10. Would you like to read some stories about Hawkeye alone?

11. Would you like to read some stories about Amy alone?

12. Which would you prefer? (Be sure to read all of the answers first. Then choose the one you like best and write the letter on your sheet.)

    12A. One long story with lots of picture clues.
    12B. One long story with only one picture clue at the end.
    12C. One long story with no picture clues at all.
    12D. A CAN YOU SOLVE THE MYSTERY?™ crime-solving kit with actual clues.
    12E. A CAN YOU SOLVE THE MYSTERY?™ video game.
    12F. A CAN YOU SOLVE THE MYSTERY?™ comic strip.
    12G. A CAN YOU SOLVE THE MYSTERY?™ comic book.

13. Who was your favorite person in the book? Why?

14. How hard were the mysteries to solve? (Write your number choice on your sheet.)

    14A. Too easy   14B. Just right   14C. Too hard

15. How hard was the book to read and understand? (Write your number choice on your sheet.)

    15A. Too easy   15B. Just right   15C. Too hard

16. Have you read any other CAN YOU SOLVE THE MYSTERY?™ books? How many? What were the titles of the books?

17. What other books do you like to read? (You can write in books that aren't mysteries, too.)

18. How old are you?

19. Are you a boy or a girl?

20. Does a CAN YOU SOLVE THE MYSTERY?™ club sound like fun?

21. Which club product do you like best? (Choose the one that is your favorite. Then write its number on your sheet.)

    21A. Membership card
    21B. T-shirt
    21C. Poster
    21D. Decoder badge
    21E. Sketch pad
    21F. Bookmark

22. Would you buy another volume of this mystery series?

HAVE YOU SOLVED ALL OF THESE EXCITING CASES?